100 Smoothie Recipes for Home

By: Kelly Johnson

Table of Contents

- Tropical Paradise
- Green Goddess
- Peanut Butter Banana Bliss
- Chocolate Almond Delight
- Mango Tango
- Detox Green Tea
- Strawberry Kiwi Cooler
- Blueberry Banana Bliss
- Cherry Vanilla
- Pineapple Mint Refresher
- Raspberry Peach Sunrise
- Coconut Avocado Dream
- Matcha Green Tea
- Blackberry Almond Bliss
- Orange Creamsicle
- Mango Basil Blast
- Cinnamon Apple Pie
- Pomegranate Berry Burst
- Choco-Banana Protein Boost
- Mint Chocolate Chip Madness
- Kiwi Berry Blast
- Turmeric Pineapple
- Cherry Almond Energy Boost
- Citrus Sunshine
- Raspberry Lemonade Cooler
- Papaya Passion
- Carrot Cake
- Blueberry Basil Bliss
- Mango Coconut Dream
- Vanilla Peach
- Cucumber Melon Cooler
- Strawberry Basil Blast
- Mocha Banana Protein
- Green Apple Ginger Zinger
- Peach Raspberry Delight
- Honeydew Mint Refresher

- Banana Blueberry Basil Boost
- Mango Turmeric Twist
- Cherry Vanilla Protein
- Tropical Green Paradise
- Pineapple Orange Burst
- Minty Watermelon Cooler
- Cocoa Berry Bliss
- Avocado Berry Boost
- Peach Ginger Energizer
- Coconut Berry Splash
- Green Detox Citrus
- Raspberry Chocolate Delight
- Mango Pineapple Sunshine
- Blueberry Spinach Powerhouse
- Strawberry Pineapple Paradise
- Cherry Almond Chocolate Bliss
- Vanilla Blueberry Oatmeal Crunch
- Kiwi Pineapple Punch
- Raspberry Mango Tango
- Cucumber Berry Refresher
- Banana Peanut Butter Crunch
- Mango Raspberry Chia Delight
- Green Tea Berry Boost
- Papaya Coconut Paradise
- Minty Mango Pineapple
- Raspberry Lemon Basil Burst
- Blackberry Lime Zest Delight
- Chocolate Avocado Dream
- Orange Carrot Ginger Elixir
- Chia Berry Protein Punch
- Strawberry Pineapple Basil Bliss
- Mango Matcha Green Tea Boost
- Peach Raspberry Oat
- Triple Berry Coconut Crush
- Banana Mango Turmeric Infusion
- Blackberry Lavender Lemonade
- Pomegranate Blueberry Burst
- Citrus Beet Detox Elixir
- Peach Basil Lemonade
- Cranberry Apple Cinnamon Spice

- Mango Raspberry Mint Marvel
- Blueberry Lemon Lavender Bliss
- Kiwi Pineapple Green Goddess
- Apricot Almond Delight
- Cinnamon Roll
- Pineapple Mint Green Goddess
- Choco-Berry Protein Delight
- Orange Ginger Carrot Crush
- Raspberry Mango Basil Bliss
- Coconut Pineapple Mint Refresher
- Strawberry Banana Chia Crunch
- Mango Basil Chia Elixir
- Blueberry Kalle Powerhouse

Tropical Paradise

- 1 cup pineapple chunks
- 1/2 cup mango chunks
- 1 banana
- 1/2 cup coconut milk
- 1/2 cup orange juice
- Ice cubes

Instructions:

Add the pineapple chunks, mango chunks, and banana to a blender.
Pour in the coconut milk and orange juice.
Add a handful of ice cubes for a refreshing chill.
Blend until smooth and creamy.
Pour into a glass and enjoy your Tropical Sunshine Smoothie!

Feel free to customize this recipe by adding other tropical fruits like papaya or passion fruit for an extra burst of flavor. Enjoy your tropical paradise in a glass!

Green Goddess

- Handful of spinach
- 1/2 cucumber, peeled and sliced
- 1/2 avocado, peeled and pitted
- 1/2 lime (juiced)
- 1 cup coconut water
- Ice cubes

Instructions:

Place spinach, cucumber, avocado, lime juice, and coconut water in a blender.
Add a handful of ice cubes to chill the smoothie.
Blend until all ingredients are well combined and the smoothie reaches your desired consistency.
Pour into a glass and enjoy the vibrant Green Goddess Smoothie!

This smoothie is not only delicious but also packed with nutrients from the greens and avocado. Feel free to adjust the quantities to suit your taste preferences. Cheers to a healthy and refreshing Green Goddess Smoothie!

Peanut Butter Banana Bliss

- 2 bananas
- 2 tablespoons peanut butter
- 1 cup milk (dairy or plant-based)
- 1/2 teaspoon cinnamon
- Ice cubes

Instructions:

Peel and slice the bananas.
Add the banana slices, peanut butter, milk, and cinnamon to a blender.
Add a handful of ice cubes for a cool and creamy texture.
Blend until all ingredients are well combined and the smoothie reaches a smooth consistency.
Pour into a glass and savor the Peanut Butter Banana Bliss!

This smoothie combines the rich flavors of peanut butter and the natural sweetness of bananas for a delightful treat. Adjust the thickness by adding more or less milk according to your preference. Enjoy this delicious and satisfying smoothie!
Chocolate Almond Delight

Chocolate Almond Delight

- 2 tablespoons cocoa powder
- 1 tablespoon almond butter
- 1 banana
- 1 cup almond milk
- 1 tablespoon honey (optional)
- Ice cubes

Instructions:

Peel and slice the banana.
In a blender, combine the banana slices, cocoa powder, almond butter, almond milk, and honey (if using).

Add a handful of ice cubes for a frosty texture.
Blend until all ingredients are well combined and the smoothie is creamy.
Pour into a glass and indulge in the Chocolate Almond Delight!

Feel free to customize the sweetness by adjusting the amount of honey or using sweetened almond milk. This smoothie offers a perfect blend of chocolate and almond flavors for a delightful treat. Enjoy!

Mango Tango

- 1 cup mango chunks
- 1/2 cup orange juice
- 1/2 cup plain yogurt
- 1 tablespoon chia seeds
- Ice cubes

Instructions:

Peel and dice the mango.
In a blender, combine the mango chunks, orange juice, plain yogurt, and chia seeds.
Add a handful of ice cubes for a refreshing chill.
Blend until the ingredients are smooth and the smoothie reaches your desired consistency.
Pour into a glass and enjoy the tropical flavors of the Mango Tango!

Feel free to customize this recipe by adding a banana for extra creaminess or a squeeze of lime for a citrusy kick. It's a delightful and nutritious way to enjoy the tropical goodness of mango. Cheers!

Detox Green Tea

- 1 green tea bag (brewed and cooled)
- Handful of spinach
- 1/2 cucumber, peeled and sliced
- 1/2 avocado, peeled and pitted
- 1/2 lime (juiced)
- 1 tablespoon honey (optional)
- Ice cubes

Instructions:

    Brew a cup of green tea and let it cool.
    In a blender, combine the cooled green tea, spinach, cucumber, avocado, lime juice, and honey (if using).
    Add a handful of ice cubes for a refreshing chill.
    Blend until the ingredients are well combined and the smoothie reaches a smooth consistency.
    Pour into a glass and enjoy the Detox Green Tea Smoothie!

This smoothie is not only hydrating but also packed with antioxidants and nutrients from the green tea and fresh greens. Adjust the sweetness with honey according to your taste preference. Cheers to a healthy and revitalizing smoothie!

Strawberry Kiwi Cooler

- 1 cup strawberries, hulled and halved
- 2 kiwis, peeled and sliced
- 1/2 cup orange juice
- 1/2 cup water
- Ice cubes

Instructions:

    Prepare the strawberries by hulling and halving them.
    Peel and slice the kiwis.
    In a blender, combine the strawberries, kiwis, orange juice, and water.
    Add a handful of ice cubes for a refreshing chill.
    Blend until all ingredients are well combined and the smoothie reaches your desired consistency.
    Pour into a glass and enjoy the vibrant and fruity Strawberry Kiwi Cooler!

Feel free to customize this recipe by adding a touch of honey or adjusting the liquid content to achieve your preferred thickness. This smoothie is a perfect combination of sweet strawberries and tart kiwi, making it a delightful and hydrating treat. Cheers!

Blueberry Banana Bliss

- 1 cup blueberries
- 1 banana

- 1/2 cup Greek yogurt
- 1 cup almond milk
- 1 tablespoon flaxseeds
- Ice cubes

Instructions:

Rinse the blueberries.
Peel and slice the banana.
In a blender, combine the blueberries, banana, Greek yogurt, almond milk, and flaxseeds.
Add a handful of ice cubes for a cool and creamy texture.
Blend until all ingredients are well combined and the smoothie reaches a smooth consistency.
Pour into a glass and savor the Blueberry Banana Bliss!

This smoothie is not only delicious but also rich in antioxidants, fiber, and healthy fats. Customize it by adding a drizzle of honey or adjusting the thickness with more or less almond milk. Enjoy this delightful and nutritious blend!

Cherry Vanilla

- 1 cup cherries (pitted)
- 1/2 cup vanilla yogurt
- 1/2 cup milk (dairy or plant-based)
- 1 tablespoon almond butter
- Ice cubes

Instructions:

Pit the cherries.
In a blender, combine the pitted cherries, vanilla yogurt, milk, and almond butter.
Add a handful of ice cubes for a refreshing chill.
Blend until all ingredients are well combined and the smoothie reaches a smooth consistency.
Pour into a glass and enjoy the Cherry Vanilla Smoothie!

Feel free to adjust the sweetness by adding a touch of honey or maple syrup if desired. This smoothie offers a perfect blend of sweet cherries and the creamy richness of vanilla. Cheers to a delicious treat!

Pineapple Mint Refresher

- 1 cup pineapple chunks
- Handful of fresh mint leaves
- 1/2 lime (juiced)
- 1/2 cup coconut water
- Ice cubes

Instructions:

> Cut pineapple into chunks.
> In a blender, combine the pineapple chunks, fresh mint leaves, lime juice, and coconut water.
> Add a handful of ice cubes for a cool and refreshing texture.
> Blend until all ingredients are well combined and the smoothie reaches a smooth consistency.
> Pour into a glass and enjoy the Pineapple Mint Refresher!

This smoothie is a perfect combination of tropical pineapple, invigorating mint, and the hydrating touch of coconut water. Adjust the sweetness or tartness by adding more or less lime juice. It's a delightful and revitalizing drink for any time of the day!

Raspberry Peach Sunrise

- 1 cup raspberries
- 1 peach (pitted and sliced)
- 1/2 cup orange juice
- 1/2 cup plain yogurt
- Ice cubes

Instructions:

> Rinse the raspberries.

Pit and slice the peach.
In a blender, combine the raspberries, sliced peach, orange juice, and plain yogurt.
Add a handful of ice cubes for a refreshing chill.
Blend until all ingredients are well combined and the smoothie reaches a smooth consistency.
Pour into a glass and enjoy the Raspberry Peach Sunrise!

Feel free to customize this recipe by adding a banana for extra creaminess or a drizzle of honey for additional sweetness. This smoothie is not only visually appealing but also a delightful combination of tart raspberries and sweet peaches. Cheers!

Coconut Avocado Dream

- 1/2 avocado
- 1/2 cup coconut milk
- 1 banana
- 1 tablespoon chia seeds
- Ice cubes

Instructions:

Peel and pit the avocado.
In a blender, combine the avocado, coconut milk, banana, and chia seeds.
Add a handful of ice cubes for a refreshing chill.
Blend until all ingredients are well combined and the smoothie reaches a creamy consistency.
Pour into a glass and enjoy the Coconut Avocado Dream!

Feel free to customize this recipe by adding a touch of honey or adjusting the thickness with more or less coconut milk. This smoothie is rich in healthy fats and provides a creamy texture with the combination of avocado and coconut milk. Enjoy the tropical flavors!

Matcha Green Tea

- 1 teaspoon matcha powder
- 1 banana
- 1/2 cup spinach
- 1/2 cup almond milk
- 1 tablespoon honey
- Ice cubes

Instructions:

In a blender, combine the matcha powder, banana, spinach, almond milk, and honey.
Add a handful of ice cubes for a refreshing chill.
Blend until all ingredients are well combined, and the smoothie reaches a smooth consistency.
Pour into a glass and savor the Matcha Green Tea Delight!

Feel free to customize this recipe by adjusting the sweetness with more or less honey. This smoothie not only provides the health benefits of matcha but also offers a vibrant green color and a delicious taste. Enjoy the energizing and antioxidant-rich goodness!

Blackberry Almond Bliss

- 1 cup blackberries
- 2 tablespoons almond butter
- 1/2 cup Greek yogurt
- 1/2 cup almond milk
- Ice cubes

Instructions:

Rinse the blackberries.
In a blender, combine the blackberries, almond butter, Greek yogurt, and almond milk.
Add a handful of ice cubes for a cool and creamy texture.
Blend until all ingredients are well combined, and the smoothie reaches a smooth consistency.
Pour into a glass and enjoy the Blackberry Almond Bliss!

Feel free to customize this recipe by adding a banana for extra creaminess or a drizzle of honey for additional sweetness. This smoothie is a delightful combination of tart blackberries and the nutty richness of almond butter. Enjoy this tasty and nutritious blend!

Orange Creamsicle

- 2 oranges (peeled and segmented)
- 1/2 cup vanilla yogurt
- 1/2 cup milk (dairy or plant-based)
- 1 tablespoon honey
- Ice cubes

Instructions:

Peel and segment the oranges.
In a blender, combine the orange segments, vanilla yogurt, milk, and honey.
Add a handful of ice cubes for a creamy and frosty texture.
Blend until all ingredients are well combined and the smoothie reaches a smooth consistency.
Pour into a glass and enjoy the Orange Creamsicle Smoothie!

Feel free to customize this recipe by adding a banana for extra creaminess or adjusting the sweetness with more or less honey. This smoothie captures the classic flavor of an orange creamsicle in a healthy and delicious drink. Cheers!

Mango Basil Blast

- 1 cup mango chunks
- Handful of fresh basil leaves
- 1/2 lemon (juiced)
- 1/2 cup coconut water
- Ice cubes

Instructions:

Peel and dice the mango.

In a blender, combine the mango chunks, fresh basil leaves, lemon juice, and coconut water.
Add a handful of ice cubes for a refreshing chill.
Blend until all ingredients are well combined and the smoothie reaches a smooth consistency.
Pour into a glass and enjoy the unique and tropical Mango Basil Blast!

This smoothie is a delightful blend of sweet mango with the aromatic and slightly peppery flavor of fresh basil. Adjust the tartness by adding more or less lemon juice according to your taste. It's a refreshing and vibrant drink to brighten up your day!

Cinnamon Apple Pie

- 1 apple (cored and sliced)
- 1/2 teaspoon cinnamon
- 1/2 cup oats
- 1/2 cup vanilla yogurt
- 1 cup almond milk
- Ice cubes

Instructions:

Core and slice the apple.
In a blender, combine the apple slices, cinnamon, oats, vanilla yogurt, and almond milk.
Add a handful of ice cubes for a refreshing chill.
Blend until all ingredients are well combined, and the smoothie reaches a smooth consistency.
Pour into a glass and enjoy the comforting and flavorful Cinnamon Apple Pie Smoothie!

Feel free to customize this recipe by adding a drizzle of honey or a sprinkle of nutmeg for additional warmth. This smoothie captures the essence of a classic apple pie with the added health benefits of oats and almond milk. Enjoy the cozy flavors!

Pomegranate Berry Burst

- 1/2 cup pomegranate seeds
- 1 cup mixed berries (strawberries, blueberries, raspberries)

- 1/2 cup Greek yogurt
- 1/2 cup water
- Ice cubes

Instructions:

> Deseed the pomegranate and set aside the seeds.
> Rinse the mixed berries.
> In a blender, combine the pomegranate seeds, mixed berries, Greek yogurt, and water.
> Add a handful of ice cubes for a refreshing chill.
> Blend until all ingredients are well combined, and the smoothie reaches a smooth consistency.
> Pour into a glass and enjoy the burst of flavors in the Pomegranate Berry Burst!

Feel free to customize this recipe by adding a banana for extra creaminess or a drizzle of honey for additional sweetness. This smoothie is not only delicious but also packed with vitamins and antioxidants from the vibrant berries and pomegranate seeds. Enjoy the refreshing and nutritious blend!

Choco-Banana Protein Boost

- 2 bananas
- 2 tablespoons chocolate protein powder
- 1 tablespoon almond butter
- 1 cup milk (dairy or plant-based)
- Ice cubes

Instructions:

> Peel and slice the bananas.
> In a blender, combine the banana slices, chocolate protein powder, almond butter, and milk.
> Add a handful of ice cubes for a cool and creamy texture.
> Blend until all ingredients are well combined, and the smoothie reaches a smooth consistency.
> Pour into a glass and enjoy the Choco-Banana Protein Boost!

Feel free to customize this recipe by adjusting the sweetness with more or less protein powder or adding a drizzle of honey. This smoothie not only satisfies your chocolate cravings but also provides a good dose of protein for a nutritious and energizing treat. Cheers!

Mint Chocolate Chip Madness

- Handful of fresh mint leaves
- 1/2 cup spinach
- 2 tablespoons cocoa powder
- 1 banana
- 1 cup almond milk
- 1 tablespoon honey or maple syrup (optional)
- 1/4 cup dark chocolate chips
- Ice cubes

Instructions:

Rinse the fresh mint leaves.
In a blender, combine the mint leaves, spinach, cocoa powder, banana, almond milk, and honey or maple syrup if using.
Add a handful of ice cubes for a refreshing chill.
Blend until all ingredients are well combined, and the smoothie reaches a smooth consistency.
Stir in the dark chocolate chips.
Pour into a glass and enjoy the Mint Chocolate Chip Madness!

Feel free to adjust the sweetness by adding more honey or maple syrup, and you can customize the texture by adding more or fewer ice cubes. This smoothie is a delightful blend of chocolate and mint, reminiscent of a classic mint chocolate chip treat. Enjoy the refreshing and decadent flavors!

Kiwi Berry Blast

- 2 kiwis, peeled and sliced
- 1 cup mixed berries (strawberries, blueberries, raspberries)
- 1/2 cup orange juice

- 1/2 cup plain yogurt
- Ice cubes

Instructions:

Peel and slice the kiwis.
Rinse the mixed berries.
In a blender, combine the kiwi slices, mixed berries, orange juice, and plain yogurt.
Add a handful of ice cubes for a refreshing chill.
Blend until all ingredients are well combined, and the smoothie reaches a smooth consistency.
Pour into a glass and enjoy the vibrant and fruity Kiwi Berry Blast!

Feel free to customize this recipe by adding a banana for extra creaminess or a drizzle of honey for additional sweetness. This smoothie is a delightful combination of tart kiwi and the sweetness of mixed berries. Enjoy the burst of flavors!

Turmeric Pineapple

- 1 cup pineapple chunks
- 1/2 teaspoon turmeric powder
- 1 banana
- 1/2 cup coconut milk
- 1 tablespoon chia seeds
- Ice cubes

Instructions:

Peel and dice the banana.
In a blender, combine the pineapple chunks, turmeric powder, diced banana, coconut milk, and chia seeds.
Add a handful of ice cubes for a refreshing chill.
Blend until all ingredients are well combined, and the smoothie reaches a smooth consistency.
Pour into a glass and enjoy the Turmeric Pineapple Smoothie!

Feel free to customize this recipe by adding a squeeze of lime for a citrusy kick or a drizzle of honey for added sweetness. This smoothie combines the tropical flavors of pineapple with the anti-inflammatory properties of turmeric for a refreshing and healthful beverage. Enjoy!

Cherry Almond Energy Boost

- 1 cup cherries (pitted)
- 2 tablespoons almond butter
- 1/2 cup vanilla yogurt
- 1 cup almond milk
- Ice cubes

Instructions:

> Pit the cherries.
> In a blender, combine the pitted cherries, almond butter, vanilla yogurt, and almond milk.
> Add a handful of ice cubes for a cool and creamy texture.
> Blend until all ingredients are well combined, and the smoothie reaches a smooth consistency.
> Pour into a glass and enjoy the Cherry Almond Energy Boost!

Feel free to customize this recipe by adding a banana for extra creaminess or a drizzle of honey for additional sweetness. This smoothie is a delightful combination of the sweet-tart flavor of cherries with the nutty richness of almond butter. It's a perfect pick-me-up for a busy day!

Citrus Sunshine

- 1 orange (peeled and segmented)
- 1/2 grapefruit (peeled and segmented)
- 1 banana
- 1/2 cup Greek yogurt
- Ice cubes

Instructions:

> Peel and segment the orange and grapefruit.
> In a blender, combine the orange segments, grapefruit segments, banana, and Greek yogurt.
> Add a handful of ice cubes for a refreshing chill.

> Blend until all ingredients are well combined, and the smoothie reaches a smooth consistency.
> Pour into a glass and enjoy the Citrus Sunshine Smoothie!

Feel free to customize this recipe by adding a touch of honey or adjusting the thickness with more or less Greek yogurt. This smoothie is a burst of citrus flavors, providing a refreshing and vitamin-packed beverage to start your day. Cheers to a sunny and delicious treat!

Raspberry Lemonade Cooler

- 1 cup raspberries
- 1/2 lemon (juiced)
- 1/2 cup coconut water
- 1 tablespoon honey
- Ice cubes

Instructions:

> Rinse the raspberries.
> Juice half a lemon.
> In a blender, combine the raspberries, lemon juice, coconut water, and honey.
> Add a handful of ice cubes for a refreshing chill.
> Blend until all ingredients are well combined, and the smoothie reaches a smooth consistency.
> Pour into a glass and enjoy the Raspberry Lemonade Cooler!

Feel free to customize this recipe by adding a slice of lemon for garnish or adjusting the sweetness with more or less honey. This smoothie is a delightful blend of tart raspberries and the zesty freshness of lemon, creating a perfect cooler for a warm day. Enjoy!

Papaya Passion

- 1 cup papaya chunks
- 1/2 cup passion fruit juice
- 1 banana
- 1/2 cup coconut milk
- Ice cubes

Instructions:

>   Peel and dice the papaya.
>   In a blender, combine the papaya chunks, passion fruit juice, banana, and coconut milk.
>   Add a handful of ice cubes for a refreshing chill.
>   Blend until all ingredients are well combined, and the smoothie reaches a smooth consistency.
>   Pour into a glass and enjoy the tropical Papaya Passion Smoothie!

Feel free to customize this recipe by adding a squeeze of lime for extra freshness or a handful of pineapple chunks for an additional tropical twist. This smoothie is a delightful mix of sweet papaya and the exotic flavor of passion fruit, creating a delicious and rejuvenating drink. Enjoy!

Carrot Cake

- 1 carrot (peeled and sliced)
- 1/2 cup oats
- 1/2 teaspoon cinnamon
- 1/2 cup vanilla yogurt
- 1 cup almond milk
- Ice cubes

Instructions:

>   Peel and slice the carrot.
>   In a blender, combine the carrot slices, oats, cinnamon, vanilla yogurt, and almond milk.
>   Add a handful of ice cubes for a refreshing chill.
>   Blend until all ingredients are well combined, and the smoothie reaches a smooth consistency.
>   Pour into a glass and enjoy the wholesome Carrot Cake Smoothie!

Feel free to customize this recipe by adding a tablespoon of nut butter for extra richness or a drizzle of maple syrup for added sweetness. This smoothie captures the flavors of carrot cake in a healthy and delicious way. Enjoy the comforting taste!

Blueberry Basil Bliss

- 1 cup blueberries
- Handful of fresh basil leaves
- 1 banana
- 1/2 cup water
- Ice cubes

Instructions:

> Rinse the blueberries.
> In a blender, combine the blueberries, fresh basil leaves, banana, and water.
> Add a handful of ice cubes for a refreshing chill.
> Blend until all ingredients are well combined, and the smoothie reaches a smooth consistency.
> Pour into a glass and enjoy the Blueberry Basil Bliss!

Feel free to customize this recipe by adding a squeeze of lime for a citrusy kick or a tablespoon of chia seeds for added texture. This smoothie is a delightful blend of sweet blueberries and the aromatic freshness of basil, creating a unique and flavorful experience. Enjoy the blissful combination!

Mango Coconut Dream

- 1 cup mango chunks
- 1/2 cup coconut milk
- 1 banana
- 1/2 cup Greek yogurt
- Ice cubes

Instructions:

> Peel and dice the banana.
> In a blender, combine the mango chunks, coconut milk, diced banana, and Greek yogurt.
> Add a handful of ice cubes for a refreshing chill.
> Blend until all ingredients are well combined, and the smoothie reaches a smooth consistency.
> Pour into a glass and enjoy the Mango Coconut Dream!

Feel free to customize this recipe by adding a tablespoon of shredded coconut for an extra coconut boost or a squeeze of lime for a citrusy twist. This smoothie is a delightful combination of tropical mango and the creamy richness of coconut, creating a dreamy and delicious beverage. Enjoy!

Vanilla Peach

- 1 cup peaches (sliced)
- 1/2 cup vanilla yogurt
- 1/2 cup milk (dairy or plant-based)
- 1 teaspoon vanilla extract
- Ice cubes

Instructions:

Slice the peaches.
In a blender, combine the sliced peaches, vanilla yogurt, milk, vanilla extract, and ice cubes.
Blend until all ingredients are well combined, and the smoothie reaches a smooth consistency.
Pour into a glass and savor the Vanilla Peach Smoothie!

Feel free to customize this recipe by adding a banana for extra creaminess or a sprinkle of cinnamon for added warmth. This smoothie captures the sweet and fragrant essence of peaches with a hint of vanilla. Enjoy the delightful flavor combination!

Cucumber Melon Cooler

- 1/2 cucumber
- 1 cup honeydew melon chunks
- 1/2 lime (juiced)
- 1/2 cup coconut water
- Ice cubes

Instructions:

Peel and slice the cucumber.

In a blender, combine the cucumber slices, honeydew melon chunks, lime juice, and coconut water.
Add a handful of ice cubes for a refreshing chill.
Blend until all ingredients are well combined, and the smoothie reaches a smooth consistency.
Pour into a glass and enjoy the Cucumber Melon Cooler!

Feel free to customize this recipe by adding a handful of mint leaves for extra freshness or a splash of sparkling water for some effervescence. This smoothie is a perfect blend of hydrating cucumber and sweet honeydew melon, creating a cool and revitalizing beverage. Enjoy!

Strawberry Basil Blast

- 1 cup strawberries (hulled and halved)
- Handful of fresh basil leaves
- 1 banana
- 1/2 cup plain yogurt
- 1/2 cup water
- Ice cubes

Instructions:

Hull and halve the strawberries.
In a blender, combine the strawberries, fresh basil leaves, banana, plain yogurt, and water.
Add a handful of ice cubes for a refreshing chill.
Blend until all ingredients are well combined, and the smoothie reaches a smooth consistency.
Pour into a glass and enjoy the Strawberry Basil Blast!

Feel free to customize this recipe by adding a squeeze of lime for a citrusy kick or a drizzle of honey for additional sweetness. This smoothie is a delightful combination of sweet strawberries and the aromatic freshness of basil, creating a unique and flavorful experience. Enjoy the blast of flavors!

Mocha Banana Protein

- 1 banana
- 1 cup brewed and cooled coffee
- 1 scoop chocolate protein powder
- 1 tablespoon almond butter
- 1/2 cup milk (dairy or plant-based)
- Ice cubes

Instructions:

Peel and slice the banana.
In a blender, combine the banana slices, brewed and cooled coffee, chocolate protein powder, almond butter, and milk.
Add a handful of ice cubes for a cool and creamy texture.
Blend until all ingredients are well combined, and the smoothie reaches a smooth consistency.
Pour into a glass and enjoy the Mocha Banana Protein smoothie!

Feel free to customize this recipe by adding a sprinkle of cocoa powder or a dash of cinnamon for extra flavor. This smoothie not only provides a boost of protein but also combines the rich flavors of coffee and chocolate for a delicious and satisfying drink. Enjoy!

Green Apple Ginger Zinger

- 1 green apple (cored and sliced)
- 1/2 inch fresh ginger (peeled and grated)
- Handful of spinach
- 1/2 lemon (juiced)
- 1 tablespoon honey
- 1 cup water
- Ice cubes

Instructions:

Core and slice the green apple.
Peel and grate the fresh ginger.

In a blender, combine the green apple slices, grated ginger, spinach, lemon juice, honey, and water.
Add a handful of ice cubes for a refreshing chill.
Blend until all ingredients are well combined, and the smoothie reaches a smooth consistency.
Pour into a glass and enjoy the Green Apple Ginger Zinger!

Feel free to customize this recipe by adjusting the sweetness with more or less honey or adding a handful of mint leaves for extra freshness. This smoothie is a zesty and revitalizing combination of green apple and ginger, providing a burst of flavor and energy. Enjoy!

Peach Raspberry Delight

- 1 cup peaches (sliced)
- 1/2 cup raspberries
- 1/2 cup Greek yogurt
- 1/2 cup almond milk
- 1 tablespoon honey
- Ice cubes

Instructions:

Slice the peaches.
Rinse the raspberries.
In a blender, combine the sliced peaches, raspberries, Greek yogurt, almond milk, and honey.
Add a handful of ice cubes for a refreshing chill.
Blend until all ingredients are well combined, and the smoothie reaches a smooth consistency.
Pour into a glass and enjoy the Peach Raspberry Delight!

Feel free to customize this recipe by adding a banana for extra creaminess or a splash of orange juice for a citrusy twist. This smoothie is a perfect blend of sweet peaches and tart raspberries, creating a delightful and nutritious beverage. Enjoy!

Honeydew Mint Refresher

- 1 cup honeydew melon chunks
- Handful of fresh mint leaves
- 1/2 lime (juiced)
- 1 tablespoon honey
- 1/2 cup coconut water
- Ice cubes

Instructions:

Cut honeydew melon into chunks.
Rinse the fresh mint leaves.
In a blender, combine the honeydew melon chunks, mint leaves, lime juice, honey, and coconut water.
Add a handful of ice cubes for a refreshing chill.
Blend until all ingredients are well combined, and the smoothie reaches a smooth consistency.
Pour into a glass and enjoy the Honeydew Mint Refresher!

Feel free to customize this recipe by adding a splash of sparkling water for some effervescence or a pinch of sea salt for a savory twist. This smoothie is a perfect balance of the sweet and juicy honeydew melon with the cool and invigorating flavor of fresh mint. Enjoy!

Banana Blueberry Basil Boost

- 1 banana
- 1/2 cup blueberries
- Handful of fresh basil leaves
- 1/2 cup Greek yogurt
- 1/2 cup almond milk
- Ice cubes

Instructions:

Peel and slice the banana.

Rinse the blueberries.
In a blender, combine the banana slices, blueberries, fresh basil leaves, Greek yogurt, and almond milk.
Add a handful of ice cubes for a refreshing chill.
Blend until all ingredients are well combined, and the smoothie reaches a smooth consistency.
Pour into a glass and enjoy the Banana Blueberry Basil Boost!

Feel free to customize this recipe by adding a drizzle of honey for extra sweetness or a squeeze of lime for a citrusy kick. This smoothie offers a delicious blend of sweet banana, tart blueberries, and the unique freshness of basil. Enjoy the boost of flavors!

Mango Turmeric Twist

- 1 cup mango chunks
- 1/2 teaspoon turmeric powder
- 1 banana
- 1/2 cup coconut milk
- 1 tablespoon chia seeds
- Ice cubes

Instructions:

Peel and dice the banana.
In a blender, combine the mango chunks, turmeric powder, diced banana, coconut milk, and chia seeds.
Add a handful of ice cubes for a refreshing chill.
Blend until all ingredients are well combined, and the smoothie reaches a smooth consistency.
Pour into a glass and enjoy the Mango Turmeric Twist!

Feel free to customize this recipe by adding a squeeze of lime for a citrusy kick or a drizzle of honey for added sweetness. This smoothie combines the tropical flavors of mango with the anti-inflammatory properties of turmeric for a refreshing and healthful beverage. Enjoy!

Cherry Vanilla Protein

- 1 cup cherries (pitted)

- 1/2 cup vanilla Greek yogurt
- 1 scoop vanilla protein powder
- 1/2 cup almond milk
- 1 tablespoon almond butter
- Ice cubes

Instructions:

Pit the cherries.
In a blender, combine the pitted cherries, vanilla Greek yogurt, vanilla protein powder, almond milk, and almond butter.
Add a handful of ice cubes for a cool and creamy texture.
Blend until all ingredients are well combined, and the smoothie reaches a smooth consistency.
Pour into a glass and enjoy the Cherry Vanilla Protein smoothie!

Feel free to customize this recipe by adding a banana for extra creaminess or adjusting the sweetness with more or less almond butter. This smoothie not only satisfies your cherry and vanilla cravings but also provides a protein boost for a nutritious and delicious beverage. Enjoy!

Tropical Green Paradise

- 1 cup pineapple chunks
- 1/2 banana
- Handful of spinach
- 1/2 cup coconut water
- Ice cubes

Instructions:

Add pineapple chunks, banana, spinach, and coconut water to a blender.
Add a handful of ice cubes for a refreshing chill.
Blend until all ingredients are well combined, and the smoothie reaches a smooth consistency.
Pour into a glass and enjoy the Tropical Green Paradise!

Feel free to customize this recipe by adding a squeeze of lime for a citrusy kick or a tablespoon of chia seeds for added texture. This smoothie combines the sweetness of pineapple with the tropical flavors of coconut and the nutritional boost from spinach. Enjoy your Tropical Green Paradise smoothie!

Pineapple Orange Burst

- 1 cup pineapple chunks
- 1 orange (peeled and segmented)
- 1/2 cup Greek yogurt
- 1/2 cup water
- Ice cubes

Instructions:

> Place pineapple chunks, peeled and segmented orange, Greek yogurt, and water in a blender.
> Add a handful of ice cubes for a refreshing chill.
> Blend until all ingredients are well combined, and the smoothie reaches a smooth consistency.
> Pour into a glass and enjoy the Pineapple Orange Burst!

Feel free to customize this recipe by adding a tablespoon of honey for extra sweetness or a handful of spinach for added nutrients. This smoothie captures the tropical sweetness of pineapple and the citrusy burst from oranges, creating a vibrant and flavorful beverage. Enjoy your Pineapple Orange Burst smoothie!

Minty Watermelon Cooler

- 2 cups watermelon chunks
- Handful of fresh mint leaves
- 1/2 lime (juiced)
- 1/2 cup coconut water
- Ice cubes

Instructions:

In a blender, combine watermelon chunks, fresh mint leaves, lime juice, and coconut water.
Add a handful of ice cubes for a refreshing chill.
Blend until all ingredients are well combined, and the smoothie reaches a smooth consistency.
Pour into a glass and enjoy the Minty Watermelon Cooler!

Feel free to customize this recipe by adding a splash of sparkling water for some effervescence or a pinch of sea salt for a savory twist. This smoothie is a perfect blend of hydrating watermelon and the cool, invigorating flavor of fresh mint. Enjoy your Minty Watermelon Cooler!

Cocoa Berry Bliss

- 1/2 cup mixed berries (strawberries, blueberries, raspberries)
- 2 tablespoons cocoa powder
- 1 banana
- 1/2 cup almond milk
- Ice cubes

Instructions:

In a blender, combine mixed berries, cocoa powder, banana, and almond milk.
Add a handful of ice cubes for a cool and creamy texture.
Blend until all ingredients are well combined, and the smoothie reaches a smooth consistency.
Pour into a glass and enjoy the Cocoa Berry Bliss!

Feel free to customize this recipe by adding a scoop of protein powder for an extra boost or a tablespoon of almond butter for added richness. This smoothie combines the rich chocolate flavor from cocoa powder with the sweetness of mixed berries, creating a delightful and satisfying treat. Enjoy your Cocoa Berry Bliss smoothie!

Avocado Berry Boost

- 1/2 avocado
- 1 cup mixed berries (strawberries, blueberries, raspberries)

- 1/2 cup Greek yogurt
- 1/2 cup almond milk
- Ice cubes

Instructions:

> Scoop out the avocado and add it to the blender.
> Add mixed berries, Greek yogurt, almond milk, and ice cubes.
> Blend until all ingredients are well combined, and the smoothie reaches a smooth consistency.
> Pour into a glass and enjoy the Avocado Berry Boost!

Feel free to customize this recipe by adding a teaspoon of honey for a touch of sweetness or a handful of spinach for an extra nutrient boost. This smoothie combines the creamy texture of avocado with the vibrant flavors of mixed berries, creating a delicious and satisfying beverage. Enjoy your Avocado Berry Boost smoothie!

Peach Ginger Energizer

- 1 cup peaches (sliced)
- 1/2 inch fresh ginger (peeled and grated)
- 1 banana
- 1/2 cup orange juice
- Ice cubes

Instructions:

> Slice the peaches.
> Peel and grate the fresh ginger.
> In a blender, combine the sliced peaches, grated ginger, banana, orange juice, and ice cubes.
> Blend until all ingredients are well combined, and the smoothie reaches a smooth consistency.
> Pour into a glass and enjoy the Peach Ginger Energizer!

Feel free to customize this recipe by adding a splash of lemon juice for an extra citrusy kick or a handful of spinach for added nutrients. This smoothie combines the sweet and juicy flavor of peaches with the zesty kick of ginger, providing a refreshing and energizing experience. Enjoy your Peach Ginger Energizer smoothie!

Coconut Berry Splash

- 1/2 cup coconut milk
- 1 cup mixed berries (strawberries, blueberries, raspberries)
- 1 banana
- Ice cubes

Instructions:

In a blender, combine coconut milk, mixed berries, banana, and ice cubes.
Blend until all ingredients are well combined, and the smoothie reaches a smooth consistency.
Pour into a glass and enjoy the Coconut Berry Splash!

Feel free to customize this recipe by adding a tablespoon of shredded coconut for extra texture or a drizzle of honey for added sweetness. This smoothie combines the creamy coconut milk with the vibrant flavors of mixed berries, creating a tropical and delightful beverage. Enjoy your Coconut Berry Splash smoothie!

Green Detox Citrus

- Handful of kale or spinach
- 1/2 cucumber
- 1 orange (peeled and segmented)
- 1/2 lemon (juiced)
- 1/2 cup coconut water
- Ice cubes

Instructions:

Rinse the kale or spinach.
Peel and slice the cucumber.
In a blender, combine the kale or spinach, cucumber, orange segments, lemon juice, coconut water, and ice cubes.
Blend until all ingredients are well combined, and the smoothie reaches a smooth consistency.
Pour into a glass and enjoy the Green Detox Citrus!

Feel free to customize this recipe by adding a knob of fresh ginger for an extra detox boost or a small apple for added sweetness. This green smoothie is packed with nutrient-rich ingredients and the refreshing citrusy flavors of orange and lemon. Enjoy your Green Detox Citrus smoothie!

Raspberry Chocolate Delight

- 1 cup raspberries
- 2 tablespoons cocoa powder
- 1/2 cup vanilla Greek yogurt
- 1/2 cup almond milk
- Ice cubes

Instructions:

Rinse the raspberries.
In a blender, combine the raspberries, cocoa powder, vanilla Greek yogurt, almond milk, and ice cubes.
Blend until all ingredients are well combined, and the smoothie reaches a smooth consistency.
Pour into a glass and enjoy the Raspberry Chocolate Delight!

Feel free to customize this recipe by adding a banana for extra creaminess or a drizzle of honey for added sweetness. This smoothie brings together the tartness of raspberries with the rich, chocolatey flavor for a delightful and indulgent treat. Enjoy your Raspberry Chocolate Delight smoothie!

Mango Pineapple Sunshine

- 1 cup mango chunks
- 1 cup pineapple chunks
- 1/2 cup vanilla yogurt
- 1/2 cup orange juice
- Ice cubes

Instructions:

In a blender, combine the mango chunks, pineapple chunks, vanilla yogurt, orange juice, and ice cubes.
Blend until all ingredients are well combined, and the smoothie reaches a smooth consistency.
Pour into a glass and enjoy the Mango Pineapple Sunshine!

Feel free to customize this recipe by adding a splash of coconut milk for extra tropical flavor or a handful of spinach for added nutrients. This smoothie is a burst of sunshine with the tropical combination of mango and pineapple, creating a refreshing and delicious beverage. Enjoy your Mango Pineapple Sunshine smoothie!

Blueberry Spinach Powerhouse

- 1 cup blueberries
- Handful of spinach
- 1 banana
- 1/2 cup Greek yogurt
- 1/2 cup almond milk
- Ice cubes

Instructions:

Rinse the blueberries.
In a blender, combine the blueberries, spinach, banana, Greek yogurt, almond milk, and ice cubes.
Blend until all ingredients are well combined, and the smoothie reaches a smooth consistency.
Pour into a glass and enjoy the Blueberry Spinach Powerhouse!

Feel free to customize this recipe by adding a tablespoon of chia seeds for added texture or a squeeze of lime for a citrusy kick. This smoothie is a nutritional powerhouse, combining the antioxidant-rich blueberries with the iron and vitamins from spinach. Enjoy your Blueberry Spinach Powerhouse smoothie!

Strawberry Pineapple Paradise

- 1 cup strawberries (hulled and halved)
- 1 cup pineapple chunks
- 1/2 cup coconut water
- 1/2 cup plain yogurt
- Ice cubes

Instructions:

> In a blender, combine the strawberries, pineapple chunks, coconut water, plain yogurt, and ice cubes.
> Blend until all ingredients are well combined, and the smoothie reaches a smooth consistency.
> Pour into a glass and enjoy the Strawberry Pineapple Paradise!

Feel free to customize this recipe by adding a tablespoon of honey for added sweetness or a handful of mint leaves for a refreshing twist. This smoothie is a tropical paradise with the sweet and tart combination of strawberries and pineapples. Enjoy your Strawberry Pineapple Paradise smoothie!

Cherry Almond Chocolate Bliss

- 1 cup cherries (pitted)
- 2 tablespoons almond butter
- 1 tablespoon cocoa powder
- 1/2 cup almond milk
- Ice cubes

Instructions:

> Pit the cherries.

In a blender, combine the pitted cherries, almond butter, cocoa powder, almond milk, and ice cubes.

Blend until all ingredients are well combined, and the smoothie reaches a smooth consistency.

Pour into a glass and enjoy the Cherry Almond Chocolate Bliss!

Feel free to customize this recipe by adding a banana for extra creaminess or a drizzle of honey for added sweetness. This smoothie combines the rich flavors of cherries, almonds, and chocolate for a truly blissful treat. Enjoy your Cherry Almond Chocolate Bliss smoothie!

Vanilla Blueberry Oatmeal Crunch

- 1/2 cup blueberries
- 1/2 cup oats
- 1/2 teaspoon vanilla extract
- 1 banana
- 1 cup milk (dairy or plant-based)
- Ice cubes

Instructions:

In a blender, combine the blueberries, oats, vanilla extract, banana, milk, and ice cubes.

Blend until all ingredients are well combined, and the smoothie reaches a smooth consistency.

Pour into a glass and enjoy the Vanilla Blueberry Oatmeal Crunch!

Feel free to customize this recipe by adding a tablespoon of almond butter for extra richness or a drizzle of maple syrup for added sweetness. This smoothie combines the goodness of blueberries and oats with the comforting flavor of vanilla, creating a satisfying and nourishing beverage. Enjoy your Vanilla Blueberry Oatmeal Crunch smoothie!

Kiwi Pineapple Punch

- 2 kiwis (peeled and sliced)
- 1 cup pineapple chunks
- 1/2 lime (juiced)
- 1/2 cup coconut water

- Ice cubes

Instructions:

> Peel and slice the kiwis.
> In a blender, combine the sliced kiwis, pineapple chunks, lime juice, coconut water, and ice cubes.
> Blend until all ingredients are well combined, and the smoothie reaches a smooth consistency.
> Pour into a glass and enjoy the Kiwi Pineapple Punch!

Feel free to customize this recipe by adding a handful of spinach for extra nutrients or a splash of ginger for a zesty kick. This smoothie combines the tropical flavors of kiwi and pineapple for a delightful and hydrating beverage. Enjoy your Kiwi Pineapple Punch smoothie!

Raspberry Mango Tango

- 1 cup raspberries
- 1 cup mango chunks
- 1/2 cup vanilla Greek yogurt
- 1/2 cup almond milk
- Ice cubes

Instructions:

> Rinse the raspberries.
> In a blender, combine the raspberries, mango chunks, vanilla Greek yogurt, almond milk, and ice cubes.
> Blend until all ingredients are well combined, and the smoothie reaches a smooth consistency.
> Pour into a glass and enjoy the Raspberry Mango Tango!

Feel free to customize this recipe by adding a banana for extra creaminess or a handful of mint leaves for a refreshing twist. This smoothie is a delightful dance of sweet raspberries and tropical mango, creating a harmonious and delicious beverage. Enjoy your Raspberry Mango Tango smoothie!

Cucumber Berry Refresher

Ingredients:

- 1/2 cucumber
- 1 cup mixed berries (strawberries, blueberries, raspberries)
- 1/2 lemon (juiced)
- 1 tablespoon honey
- 1/2 cup water
- Ice cubes

Instructions:

Peel and slice the cucumber.
In a blender, combine the cucumber slices, mixed berries, lemon juice, honey, water, and ice cubes.
Blend until all ingredients are well combined, and the smoothie reaches a smooth consistency.
Pour into a glass and enjoy the Cucumber Berry Refresher!

Feel free to customize this recipe by adding a handful of spinach for extra nutrients or a splash of mint for a burst of freshness. This smoothie combines the crispness of cucumber with the sweetness of mixed berries for a revitalizing and flavorful beverage. Enjoy your Cucumber Berry Refresher smoothie!

Banana Peanut Butter Crunch

- 2 bananas
- 2 tablespoons peanut butter
- 1/2 cup oats
- 1 cup milk (dairy or plant-based)
- Ice cubes

Instructions:

Peel and slice the bananas.
In a blender, combine the sliced bananas, peanut butter, oats, milk, and ice cubes.
Blend until all ingredients are well combined, and the smoothie reaches a smooth consistency.

Pour into a glass and enjoy the Banana Peanut Butter Crunch!

Feel free to customize this recipe by adding a scoop of protein powder for an extra boost or a drizzle of honey for added sweetness. This smoothie combines the classic combination of bananas and peanut butter with the heartiness of oats, creating a creamy and satisfying beverage. Enjoy your Banana Peanut Butter Crunch smoothie!

Mango Raspberry Chia Delight

- 1 cup mango chunks
- 1/2 cup raspberries
- 1 tablespoon chia seeds
- 1/2 cup coconut milk
- Ice cubes

Instructions:

In a blender, combine the mango chunks, raspberries, chia seeds, coconut milk, and ice cubes.
Blend until all ingredients are well combined, and the smoothie reaches a smooth consistency.
Pour into a glass and enjoy the Mango Raspberry Chia Delight!

Feel free to customize this recipe by adding a splash of lime juice for a citrusy kick or a drizzle of honey for added sweetness. This smoothie combines the tropical sweetness of mango with the tartness of raspberries and the added texture of chia seeds for a delightful and satisfying treat. Enjoy your Mango Raspberry Chia Delight smoothie!

Green Tea Berry Boost

- 1 cup mixed berries (strawberries, blueberries, raspberries)
- 1 teaspoon matcha green tea powder
- 1/2 cup vanilla Greek yogurt
- 1/2 cup almond milk
- Ice cubes

Instructions:

In a blender, combine the mixed berries, matcha green tea powder, vanilla Greek yogurt, almond milk, and ice cubes.
Blend until all ingredients are well combined, and the smoothie reaches a smooth consistency.
Pour into a glass and enjoy the Green Tea Berry Boost!

Feel free to customize this recipe by adding a banana for extra creaminess or a handful of spinach for added nutrients. This smoothie combines the antioxidant-rich properties of green tea with the vibrant flavors of mixed berries for a refreshing and healthful beverage. Enjoy your Green Tea Berry Boost smoothie!

Papaya Coconut Paradise

- 1 cup papaya chunks
- 1/2 cup coconut milk
- 1/2 banana
- 1/2 cup Greek yogurt
- Ice cubes

Instructions:

In a blender, combine the papaya chunks, coconut milk, banana, Greek yogurt, and ice cubes.
Blend until all ingredients are well combined, and the smoothie reaches a smooth consistency.
Pour into a glass and enjoy the Papaya Coconut Paradise!

Feel free to customize this recipe by adding a squeeze of lime for a citrusy kick or a tablespoon of shredded coconut for added texture. This smoothie combines the tropical sweetness of papaya with the creamy richness of coconut for a delightful and hydrating beverage. Enjoy your Papaya Coconut Paradise smoothie!

Minty Mango Pineapple

- 1 cup mango chunks
- 1 cup pineapple chunks
- Handful of fresh mint leaves
- 1/2 lime (juiced)
- 1/2 cup coconut water

- Ice cubes

Instructions:

> In a blender, combine the mango chunks, pineapple chunks, fresh mint leaves, lime juice, coconut water, and ice cubes.
> Blend until all ingredients are well combined, and the smoothie reaches a smooth consistency.
> Pour into a glass and enjoy the Minty Mango Pineapple!

Feel free to customize this recipe by adding a tablespoon of honey for extra sweetness or a handful of spinach for added nutrients. This smoothie is a delightful blend of tropical mango and pineapple with the cool, invigorating flavor of mint. Enjoy your Minty Mango Pineapple smoothie!

Raspberry Lemon Basil Burst

- 1 cup raspberries
- 1/2 lemon (juiced)
- Handful of fresh basil leaves
- 1/2 cup water
- Ice cubes

Instructions:

> In a blender, combine the raspberries, freshly squeezed lemon juice, fresh basil leaves, water, and ice cubes.
> Blend until all ingredients are well combined, and the smoothie reaches a smooth consistency.
> Pour into a glass and enjoy the Raspberry Lemon Basil Burst!

Feel free to customize this recipe by adding a tablespoon of chia seeds for added texture or a drizzle of honey for extra sweetness. This smoothie is a burst of fruity, citrusy, and herbal flavors, making it a refreshing and delightful beverage. Enjoy your Raspberry Lemon Basil Burst smoothie!

Blackberry Lime Zest Delight

- 1 cup blackberries
- Zest of 1 lime

- 1/2 lime (juiced)
- 1/2 cup vanilla Greek yogurt
- 1/2 cup coconut water
- Ice cubes

Instructions:

In a blender, combine the blackberries, lime zest, freshly squeezed lime juice, vanilla Greek yogurt, coconut water, and ice cubes.
Blend until all ingredients are well combined, and the smoothie reaches a smooth consistency.
Pour into a glass and enjoy the Blackberry Lime Zest Delight!

Feel free to customize this recipe by adding a handful of spinach for added nutrients or a tablespoon of chia seeds for extra texture. This smoothie combines the bold flavor of blackberries with the zesty kick of lime zest for a delightful and invigorating beverage. Enjoy your Blackberry Lime Zest Delight smoothie!

Chocolate Avocado Dream

- 1 ripe avocado
- 2 tablespoons cocoa powder
- 1 banana
- 1/2 cup almond milk
- Ice cubes

Instructions:

Peel and pit the ripe avocado.
In a blender, combine the avocado, cocoa powder, banana, almond milk, and ice cubes.
Blend until all ingredients are well combined, and the smoothie reaches a smooth consistency.
Pour into a glass and enjoy the Chocolate Avocado Dream!

Feel free to customize this recipe by adding a scoop of chocolate protein powder for an extra boost or a drizzle of honey for added sweetness. This smoothie combines the creamy texture of avocado with the rich, indulgent flavor of chocolate for a dreamy and satisfying beverage. Enjoy your Chocolate Avocado Dream smoothie!

Orange Carrot Ginger Elixir

- 2 oranges (peeled and segmented)
- 1 carrot (peeled and sliced)
- 1/2 inch fresh ginger (peeled and grated)
- 1/2 cup orange juice
- 1/2 cup water
- Ice cubes

Instructions:

> Peel and segment the oranges.
> Peel and slice the carrot.
> In a blender, combine the orange segments, sliced carrot, grated ginger, orange juice, water, and ice cubes.
> Blend until all ingredients are well combined, and the smoothie reaches a smooth consistency.
> Pour into a glass and enjoy the Orange Carrot Ginger Elixir!

Feel free to customize this recipe by adding a splash of lemon juice for extra citrusy flavor or a pinch of turmeric for an anti-inflammatory boost. This smoothie is a vibrant and healthful elixir with the sweet and tangy combination of oranges, the earthy sweetness of carrots, and the warming kick of fresh ginger. Enjoy your Orange Carrot Ginger Elixir smoothie!

Chia Berry Protein Punch

- 1 cup mixed berries (strawberries, blueberries, raspberries)
- 1 tablespoon chia seeds
- 1 scoop vanilla protein powder
- 1/2 cup Greek yogurt
- 1/2 cup almond milk
- Ice cubes

Instructions:

In a blender, combine the mixed berries, chia seeds, vanilla protein powder, Greek yogurt, almond milk, and ice cubes.
Blend until all ingredients are well combined, and the smoothie reaches a smooth consistency.
Pour into a glass and enjoy the Chia Berry Protein Punch!

Feel free to customize this recipe by adding a banana for extra creaminess or a drizzle of honey for added sweetness. This smoothie is a delicious and protein-rich option, combining the goodness of mixed berries with the nutritional benefits of chia seeds and protein powder. Enjoy your Chia Berry Protein Punch smoothie!

Strawberry Pineapple Basil Bliss

- 1 cup strawberries (hulled and halved)
- 1 cup pineapple chunks
- Handful of fresh basil leaves
- 1/2 cup coconut water
- Ice cubes

Instructions:

In a blender, combine the strawberries, pineapple chunks, fresh basil leaves, coconut water, and ice cubes.
Blend until all ingredients are well combined, and the smoothie reaches a smooth consistency.
Pour into a glass and enjoy the Strawberry Pineapple Basil Bliss!

Feel free to customize this recipe by adding a splash of lime juice for a citrusy kick or a drizzle of honey for added sweetness. This smoothie is a delightful fusion of sweet strawberries, tropical pineapple, and the aromatic essence of fresh basil. Enjoy your Strawberry Pineapple Basil Bliss smoothie!

Mango Matcha Green Tea Boost

- 1 cup mango chunks

- 1 teaspoon matcha green tea powder
- 1/2 cup Greek yogurt
- 1/2 cup almond milk
- Ice cubes

Instructions:

In a blender, combine the mango chunks, matcha green tea powder, Greek yogurt, almond milk, and ice cubes.
Blend until all ingredients are well combined, and the smoothie reaches a smooth consistency.
Pour into a glass and enjoy the Mango Matcha Green Tea Boost!

Feel free to customize this recipe by adding a banana for extra creaminess or a drizzle of honey for added sweetness. This smoothie combines the tropical sweetness of mango with the vibrant and earthy flavors of matcha green tea for a refreshing and healthful beverage. Enjoy your Mango Matcha Green Tea Boost smoothie!

Peach Raspberry Oat

- 1 cup peaches (sliced)
- 1/2 cup raspberries
- 1/2 cup rolled oats
- 1/2 cup Greek yogurt
- 1/2 cup almond milk
- Ice cubes

Instructions:

In a blender, combine the sliced peaches, raspberries, rolled oats, Greek yogurt, almond milk, and ice cubes.
Blend until all ingredients are well combined, and the smoothie reaches a smooth consistency.
Pour into a glass and enjoy the Peach Raspberry Oat!

Feel free to customize this recipe by adding a tablespoon of chia seeds for added texture or a drizzle of maple syrup for extra sweetness. This smoothie is a delightful blend of sweet peaches, tart raspberries, and the heartiness of oats for a satisfying and nutritious beverage. Enjoy your Peach Raspberry Oat smoothie!

Triple Berry Coconut Crush

- 1/2 cup strawberries (hulled and halved)
- 1/2 cup blueberries
- 1/2 cup raspberries
- 1/2 cup coconut milk
- 1/2 cup Greek yogurt
- Ice cubes

Instructions:

In a blender, combine the strawberries, blueberries, raspberries, coconut milk, Greek yogurt, and ice cubes.
Blend until all ingredients are well combined, and the smoothie reaches a smooth consistency.
Pour into a glass and enjoy the Triple Berry Coconut Crush!

Feel free to customize this recipe by adding a squeeze of lime for a citrusy kick or a tablespoon of shredded coconut for added texture. This smoothie is a delightful blend of three berries with the tropical richness of coconut, creating a refreshing and satisfying beverage. Enjoy your Triple Berry Coconut Crush smoothie!

Banana Mango Turmeric Infusion

- 1 banana
- 1 cup mango chunks
- 1/2 teaspoon ground turmeric
- 1/2 cup Greek yogurt
- 1/2 cup almond milk
- Ice cubes

Instructions:

> In a blender, combine the banana, mango chunks, ground turmeric, Greek yogurt, almond milk, and ice cubes.
> Blend until all ingredients are well combined, and the smoothie reaches a smooth consistency.
> Pour into a glass and enjoy the Banana Mango Turmeric Infusion!

Feel free to customize this recipe by adding a dash of black pepper to enhance the absorption of turmeric or a teaspoon of honey for added sweetness. This smoothie combines the tropical flavors of banana and mango with the anti-inflammatory properties of turmeric for a refreshing and healthful beverage. Enjoy your Banana Mango Turmeric Infusion smoothie!

Blackberry Lavender Lemonade

- 1 cup blackberries
- 1 tablespoon dried culinary lavender buds (ensure they are food-grade)
- Juice of 1 lemon
- 1-2 tablespoons honey or agave syrup (adjust to taste)
- 1/2 cup Greek yogurt
- 1/2 cup water
- Ice cubes

Instructions:

> In a blender, combine the blackberries, dried lavender buds, lemon juice, honey or agave syrup, Greek yogurt, water, and ice cubes.
> Blend until all ingredients are well combined, and the smoothie reaches a smooth consistency.
> Strain the mixture through a fine mesh sieve to remove lavender buds, if desired, or leave them for added texture and flavor.
> Pour into a glass and enjoy the Blackberry Lavender Lemonade!

This smoothie combines the sweet and tart flavors of blackberries and lemon with the aromatic essence of lavender, creating a unique and refreshing beverage. Adjust the sweetness to your liking and savor the delightful combination of flavors. Enjoy your Blackberry Lavender Lemonade smoothie!

Pomegranate Blueberry Burst

- 1/2 cup pomegranate seeds
- 1/2 cup blueberries
- 1/2 cup vanilla Greek yogurt
- 1/2 cup pomegranate juice
- Ice cubes

Instructions:

In a blender, combine the pomegranate seeds, blueberries, vanilla Greek yogurt, pomegranate juice, and ice cubes.
Blend until all ingredients are well combined, and the smoothie reaches a smooth consistency.
Pour into a glass and enjoy the Pomegranate Blueberry Burst!

Feel free to customize this recipe by adding a handful of spinach for added nutrients or a drizzle of honey for extra sweetness. This smoothie is bursting with the sweet and tangy flavors of pomegranate and blueberries, providing a refreshing and nutritious beverage. Enjoy your Pomegranate Blueberry Burst smoothie!

Citrus Beet Detox Elixir

- 1 small beet (peeled and chopped)
- 1 orange (peeled and segmented)
- 1/2 grapefruit (peeled and segmented)
- 1/2 lemon (juiced)
- 1 tablespoon chia seeds
- 1/2 cup coconut water
- Ice cubes

Instructions:

In a blender, combine the chopped beet, orange segments, grapefruit segments, lemon juice, chia seeds, coconut water, and ice cubes.
Blend until all ingredients are well combined, and the smoothie reaches a smooth consistency.

Pour into a glass and enjoy the Citrus Beet Detox Elixir!

Feel free to customize this recipe by adding a handful of mint leaves for a refreshing twist or a knob of ginger for added zing. This smoothie combines the vibrant colors and detoxifying properties of beets with the citrusy goodness of oranges, grapefruit, and lemon for a revitalizing and healthful elixir. Enjoy your Citrus Beet Detox Elixir smoothie!

Peach Basil Lemonade

- 1 cup peaches (sliced)
- Handful of fresh basil leaves
- Juice of 1 lemon
- 1-2 tablespoons honey or agave syrup (adjust to taste)
- 1/2 cup Greek yogurt
- 1/2 cup water
- Ice cubes

Instructions:

In a blender, combine the sliced peaches, fresh basil leaves, lemon juice, honey or agave syrup, Greek yogurt, water, and ice cubes.
Blend until all ingredients are well combined, and the smoothie reaches a smooth consistency.
Pour into a glass and enjoy the Peach Basil Lemonade!

Feel free to customize this recipe by adding a splash of sparkling water for extra fizziness or a few slices of cucumber for a cooling effect. This smoothie brings together the sweetness of peaches, the herbal essence of basil, and the tartness of lemon for a delightful and flavorful beverage. Enjoy your Peach Basil Lemonade smoothie!

Cranberry Apple Cinnamon Spice

- 1/2 cup cranberries (fresh or frozen)
- 1 apple (cored and sliced)
- 1/2 teaspoon ground cinnamon
- 1/4 teaspoon ground nutmeg
- 1 tablespoon honey or maple syrup (adjust to taste)
- 1/2 cup vanilla Greek yogurt
- 1/2 cup apple juice

- Ice cubes

Instructions:

In a blender, combine the cranberries, apple slices, ground cinnamon, ground nutmeg, honey or maple syrup, vanilla Greek yogurt, apple juice, and ice cubes. Blend until all ingredients are well combined, and the smoothie reaches a smooth consistency.
Pour into a glass and enjoy the Cranberry Apple Cinnamon Spice!

Feel free to customize this recipe by adding a pinch of cloves for extra warmth or a handful of spinach for added nutrients. This smoothie is a delightful blend of seasonal flavors, combining the tartness of cranberries, the sweetness of apples, and the warming spices of cinnamon and nutmeg. Enjoy your Cranberry Apple Cinnamon Spice smoothie!

Mango Raspberry Mint Marvel

- 1 cup mango chunks
- 1/2 cup raspberries
- Handful of fresh mint leaves
- 1/2 lime (juiced)
- 1/2 cup coconut water
- Ice cubes

Instructions:

In a blender, combine the mango chunks, raspberries, fresh mint leaves, lime juice, coconut water, and ice cubes.
Blend until all ingredients are well combined, and the smoothie reaches a smooth consistency.
Pour into a glass and enjoy the Mango Raspberry Mint Marvel!

Feel free to customize this recipe by adding a splash of pineapple juice for extra tropical sweetness or a teaspoon of chia seeds for added texture. This smoothie is a burst of fruity goodness with the tropical flavor of mango, the tartness of raspberries, and the refreshing kick of mint. Enjoy your Mango Raspberry Mint Marvel smoothie!

Blueberry Lemon Lavender Bliss

- 1 cup blueberries
- Zest of 1 lemon
- Juice of 1/2 lemon
- 1 tablespoon dried culinary lavender buds (ensure they are food-grade)
- 1/2 cup vanilla Greek yogurt
- 1/2 cup almond milk
- Ice cubes

Instructions:

In a blender, combine the blueberries, lemon zest, lemon juice, dried lavender buds, vanilla Greek yogurt, almond milk, and ice cubes.
Blend until all ingredients are well combined, and the smoothie reaches a smooth consistency.
Strain the mixture through a fine mesh sieve to remove lavender buds, if desired, or leave them for added texture and flavor.
Pour into a glass and enjoy the Blueberry Lemon Lavender Bliss!

Feel free to customize this recipe by adding a teaspoon of honey for extra sweetness or a handful of spinach for added nutrients. This smoothie combines the sweet and tart flavors of blueberries and lemon with the floral notes of lavender, creating a blissful and aromatic beverage. Enjoy your Blueberry Lemon Lavender Bliss smoothie!

Kiwi Pineapple Green Goddess

- 2 kiwis (peeled and sliced)
- 1 cup pineapple chunks
- Handful of spinach leaves
- 1/2 avocado
- 1/2 lime (juiced)
- 1/2 cup coconut water
- Ice cubes

Instructions:

In a blender, combine the sliced kiwis, pineapple chunks, spinach leaves, avocado, lime juice, coconut water, and ice cubes.
Blend until all ingredients are well combined, and the smoothie reaches a smooth consistency.
Pour into a glass and enjoy the Kiwi Pineapple Green Goddess!

Feel free to customize this recipe by adding a handful of cilantro or mint for an extra burst of freshness or a tablespoon of chia seeds for added texture. This smoothie is a green powerhouse with the tropical flavors of kiwi and pineapple, combined with the nutrient-rich goodness of spinach and avocado. Enjoy your Kiwi Pineapple Green Goddess smoothie!

Apricot Almond Delight

- 1 cup apricots (fresh or dried, pits removed)
- 2 tablespoons almond butter
- 1/2 cup vanilla Greek yogurt
- 1/2 cup almond milk
- 1 tablespoon honey (optional, for sweetness)
- Ice cubes

Instructions:

If using fresh apricots, pit and slice them. If using dried apricots, ensure the pits are removed.
In a blender, combine the apricots, almond butter, vanilla Greek yogurt, almond milk, honey (if using), and ice cubes.

Blend until all ingredients are well combined, and the smoothie reaches a smooth consistency.
Pour into a glass and enjoy the Apricot Almond Delight!

Feel free to customize this recipe by adding a sprinkle of cinnamon for extra warmth or a tablespoon of oats for added fiber. This smoothie combines the sweet and slightly tart flavor of apricots with the nutty richness of almond butter for a delightful and satisfying beverage. Enjoy your Apricot Almond Delight smoothie!

Cinnamon Roll

- 1 banana
- 1/2 cup rolled oats
- 1/2 teaspoon ground cinnamon
- 1 tablespoon almond butter
- 1/2 cup vanilla Greek yogurt
- 1/2 cup milk (dairy or plant-based)
- 1 tablespoon honey or maple syrup (optional, for sweetness)
- Ice cubes

Instructions:

In a blender, combine the banana, rolled oats, ground cinnamon, almond butter, vanilla Greek yogurt, milk, honey or maple syrup (if using), and ice cubes.
Blend until all ingredients are well combined, and the smoothie reaches a smooth consistency.
Pour into a glass and enjoy the Cinnamon Roll smoothie!

Feel free to customize this recipe by adding a dash of nutmeg for extra warmth or a sprinkle of chopped nuts on top for added crunch. This smoothie captures the cozy and comforting flavors of a cinnamon roll while providing a nutritious and filling treat. Enjoy your Cinnamon Roll smoothie!

Pineapple Mint Green Goddess

- 1 cup pineapple chunks
- Handful of fresh mint leaves

- 1/2 cucumber (peeled and sliced)
- 1/2 lime (juiced)
- 1/2 avocado
- 1/2 cup coconut water
- Ice cubes

Instructions:

In a blender, combine the pineapple chunks, fresh mint leaves, sliced cucumber, lime juice, avocado, coconut water, and ice cubes.
Blend until all ingredients are well combined, and the smoothie reaches a smooth consistency.
Pour into a glass and enjoy the Pineapple Mint Green Goddess!

Feel free to customize this recipe by adding a handful of spinach for an extra boost of green goodness or a teaspoon of chia seeds for added texture. This smoothie is a vibrant and hydrating blend of tropical pineapple, refreshing mint, and the nutrient-rich goodness of cucumber and avocado. Enjoy your Pineapple Mint Green Goddess smoothie!

Choco-Berry Protein Delight

- 1 cup mixed berries (strawberries, blueberries, raspberries)
- 1 scoop chocolate protein powder
- 1 tablespoon almond butter
- 1/2 cup Greek yogurt
- 1/2 cup almond milk
- Ice cubes

Instructions:

In a blender, combine the mixed berries, chocolate protein powder, almond butter, Greek yogurt, almond milk, and ice cubes.
Blend until all ingredients are well combined, and the smoothie reaches a smooth consistency.
Pour into a glass and enjoy the Choco-Berry Protein Delight!

Feel free to customize this recipe by adding a banana for extra creaminess or a drizzle of honey for added sweetness. This smoothie combines the antioxidant-rich berries with the indulgent flavor of chocolate protein powder and the creaminess of almond butter, creating a delightful and nutritious beverage. Enjoy your Choco-Berry Protein Delight smoothie!

Orange Ginger Carrot Crush

- 1 orange (peeled and segmented)
- 1 carrot (peeled and sliced)
- 1/2 inch fresh ginger (peeled and grated)
- 1/2 lemon (juiced)
- 1 tablespoon honey or agave syrup (optional, for sweetness)
- 1/2 cup Greek yogurt
- 1/2 cup water
- Ice cubes

Instructions:

In a blender, combine the orange segments, sliced carrot, grated ginger, lemon juice, honey or agave syrup (if using), Greek yogurt, water, and ice cubes.
Blend until all ingredients are well combined, and the smoothie reaches a smooth consistency.
Pour into a glass and enjoy the Orange Ginger Carrot Crush!

Feel free to customize this recipe by adding a pinch of turmeric for an anti-inflammatory boost or a handful of mint leaves for extra freshness. This smoothie is a vibrant and healthful blend of citrusy orange, spicy ginger, and the earthy sweetness of carrots. Enjoy your Orange Ginger Carrot Crush smoothie!

Raspberry Mango Basil Bliss

- 1 cup raspberries
- 1 cup mango chunks
- Handful of fresh basil leaves
- 1/2 lime (juiced)
- 1/2 cup coconut water
- Ice cubes

Instructions:

In a blender, combine the raspberries, mango chunks, fresh basil leaves, lime juice, coconut water, and ice cubes.
Blend until all ingredients are well combined, and the smoothie reaches a smooth consistency.
Pour into a glass and enjoy the Raspberry Mango Basil Bliss!

Feel free to customize this recipe by adding a splash of orange juice for extra citrusy sweetness or a tablespoon of chia seeds for added texture. This smoothie is a refreshing combination of sweet raspberries, tropical mango, and the aromatic essence of fresh basil. Enjoy your Raspberry Mango Basil Bliss smoothie!

Coconut Pineapple Mint Refresher

- 1 cup pineapple chunks
- 1/2 cup coconut milk
- Handful of fresh mint leaves
- 1/2 lime (juiced)
- 1 tablespoon honey or agave syrup (optional, for sweetness)
- 1/2 cup Greek yogurt
- Ice cubes

Instructions:

In a blender, combine the pineapple chunks, coconut milk, fresh mint leaves, lime juice, honey or agave syrup (if using), Greek yogurt, and ice cubes.
Blend until all ingredients are well combined, and the smoothie reaches a smooth consistency.
Pour into a glass and enjoy the Coconut Pineapple Mint Refresher!

Feel free to customize this recipe by adding a handful of spinach for an extra nutrient boost or a splash of coconut water for a lighter texture. This smoothie is a tropical delight, combining the sweetness of pineapple with the creamy richness of coconut and the refreshing kick of mint. Enjoy your Coconut Pineapple Mint Refresher smoothie!

Strawberry Banana Chia Crunch

- 1 cup strawberries (hulled and halved)
- 1 banana
- 1 tablespoon chia seeds

- 1/4 cup rolled oats
- 1/2 cup Greek yogurt
- 1/2 cup almond milk
- Ice cubes

Instructions:

In a blender, combine the strawberries, banana, chia seeds, rolled oats, Greek yogurt, almond milk, and ice cubes.
Blend until all ingredients are well combined, and the smoothie reaches a smooth consistency.
Pour into a glass and enjoy the Strawberry Banana Chia Crunch!

Feel free to customize this recipe by adding a drizzle of honey for extra sweetness or a handful of granola on top for added crunch. This smoothie is a delightful combination of sweet strawberries, creamy banana, and the crunchiness of chia seeds and oats. Enjoy your Strawberry Banana Chia Crunch smoothie!

Mango Basil Chia Elixir

- 1 cup mango chunks
- Handful of fresh basil leaves
- 1 tablespoon chia seeds
- 1/2 lemon (juiced)
- 1/2 cup coconut water
- 1/2 cup Greek yogurt
- Ice cubes

Instructions:

In a blender, combine the mango chunks, fresh basil leaves, chia seeds, lemon juice, coconut water, Greek yogurt, and ice cubes.
Blend until all ingredients are well combined, and the smoothie reaches a smooth consistency.
Pour into a glass and enjoy the Mango Basil Chia Elixir!

Feel free to customize this recipe by adding a splash of pineapple juice for extra sweetness or a handful of spinach for an additional nutrient boost. This smoothie is a delightful fusion of tropical mango, aromatic basil, and the healthful benefits of chia seeds. Enjoy your Mango Basil Chia Elixir smoothie!

Blueberry Kalle Powerhouse

- 1 cup blueberries
- Handful of fresh kale leaves (stems removed)
- 1 banana
- 1 tablespoon flaxseeds
- 1/2 cup Greek yogurt
- 1/2 cup almond milk
- Ice cubes

Instructions:

In a blender, combine the blueberries, fresh kale leaves, banana, flaxseeds, Greek yogurt, almond milk, and ice cubes.
Blend until all ingredients are well combined, and the smoothie reaches a smooth consistency.
Pour into a glass and enjoy the Blueberry Kale Powerhouse!

Feel free to customize this recipe by adding a scoop of protein powder for an extra protein boost or a drizzle of honey for added sweetness. This smoothie is a nutritional powerhouse, combining the antioxidant-rich blueberries, leafy green kale, and the healthful benefits of flaxseeds. Enjoy your Blueberry Kale Powerhouse smoothie!

www.ingramcontent.com/pod-product-compliance
Lightning Source LLC
LaVergne TN
LVHW081320060526
838201LV00055B/2383